1966

YEARBOOK

INDEX

People In High Office

Monarch - Elizabeth II

Prime Minister
16th October 1964
- 19th June 1970

President
22nd November 1963
- 20th January 1969

Harold Wilson
Labour Party

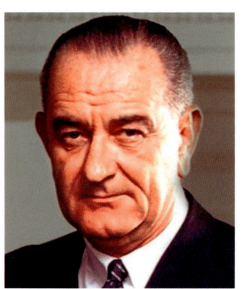

Lyndon B. Johnsonn
Democratic Party

Australia

Prime Ministers
Sir Robert Menzies
Harold Holt

Brazil

President
Humberto de Alencar Castelo
Branco

Canada

Prime Minister
Lester B. Pearson

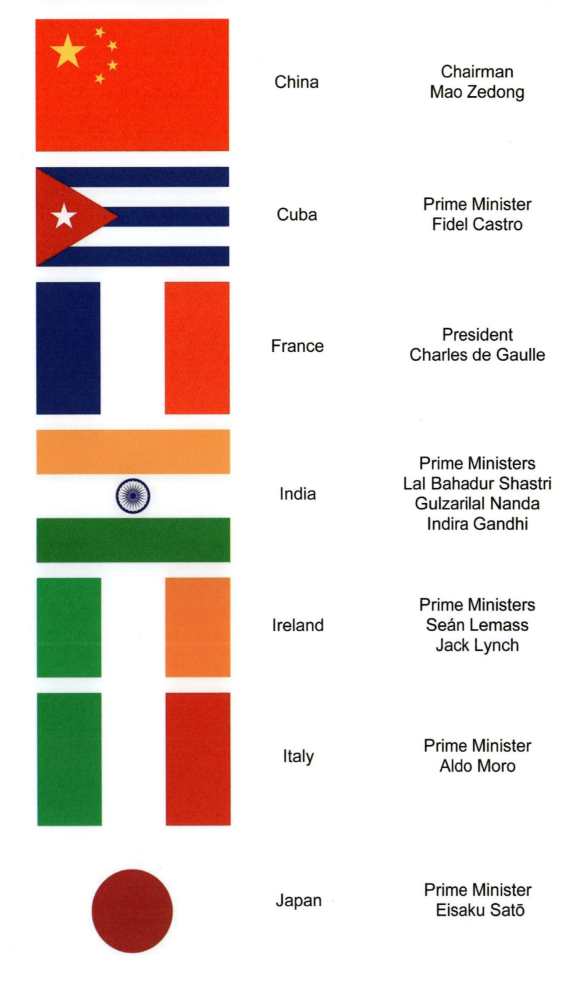

China — Chairman Mao Zedong

Cuba — Prime Minister Fidel Castro

France — President Charles de Gaulle

India — Prime Ministers Lal Bahadur Shastri Gulzarilal Nanda Indira Gandhi

Ireland — Prime Ministers Seán Lemass Jack Lynch

Italy — Prime Minister Aldo Moro

Japan — Prime Minister Eisaku Satō

Mexico

President
Gustavo Díaz Ordaz

New Zealand

Prime Minister
Keith Holyoake

Pakistan

President
Ayub Khan

Spain

President
Francisco Franco

Soviet Union

Communist Party Leader
Leonid Brezhnev

South Africa

Prime Ministers
Hendrik Verwoerd
Theophilus 'Eben' Dönges
B. J. Vorster

West
Germany

Chancellors
Ludwig Erhard
Kurt Georg Kiesinger

EVENTS FROM 1966

JANUARY

3rd   British Rail begins its full electric passenger train services over the West Coast Main Line from Euston to Manchester and Liverpool with a 100mph operation from London to Rugby. Services were officially inaugurated on the 18th April.

Stop-motion children's television series Camberwick Green had its first showing on BBC1. There were eventually 13 fifteen-minute colour episodes produced by Gordon Murray Pictures.

4th   More than 4,000 people attend a memorial service at Westminster Abbey for the broadcaster Richard Dimbleby who died on the 22nd December 1965 aged just 52.

12th   Three British MPs visiting Rhodesia (Christopher Rowland, Jeremy Bray and David Ennals) are assaulted by supporters of Rhodesian Prime Minister Ian Smith.

20th   The Queen commutes the death sentence on a black prisoner in Rhodesia two months after its abolition in Britain.

Radio Caroline South pirate radio ship MV Mi Amigo runs aground on the beach at Frinton.

21st   The Smith regime in Rhodesia rejects the Royal Prerogative commuting death sentences on two Africans.

31st   United Kingdom ceases all trade with Rhodesia.

Radio Caroline pirate radio ship MV Mi Amigo runs aground

FEBRUARY

9th   A prototype Fast Reactor nuclear reactor opens at Dounreay on the north coast of Scotland.

17th   Britain protests to South Africa over its supplying of petrol to Rhodesia.

FEBRUARY

19th	Naval minister Christopher Mayhew resigns after the government decided to shift British airpower from carrier-based planes to land-based planes and cancel the CVA-01 aircraft carrier programme.
28th	Harold Wilson calls a general election for the 31st March in the hope of increasing his single-seat majority.

Pickles shows where he found the World Cup Trophy and again receiving his reward

MARCH

1st	Chancellor of the Exchequer James Callaghan announces the decision to embrace decimalisation of the pound (which was to be effected on the 15th February 1971).
4th	In an interview published in The Evening Standard John Lennon of The Beatles commented, "We're more popular than Jesus now". Britain recognises the new regime in Ghana.
5th	BOAC Flight 911 crashes in severe clear-air turbulence over Mount Fuji after taking off from Tokyo International Airport in Japan. All 124 on board were killed.
9th	Ronnie Kray shoots George Cornell dead at The Blind Beggar pub in Whitechapel, East London. Cornell was an associate of rivals The Richardson Gang. Kray was finally convicted in 1969.
11th	Chi-Chi (London Zoo's giant panda) is flown to Moscow for a union with An-An from the Moscow Zoo.
20th	The FIFA World Cup Trophy is stolen whilst on exhibition in London.
23rd	Pope Paul VI and the Archbishop of Canterbury Michael Ramsey meet in Rome.
27th	A mongrel dog called Pickles finds the FIFA World Cup Trophy wrapped in newspaper in a South London garden.
31st	The Labour Party under Harold Wilson win the general election with a majority of 96 seats. At the 1964 election they had a majority of five but subsequent by-election defeats had led to that being reduced to just one seat before the election.

APRIL

6th   Hoverlloyd inaugurate the first Cross-Channel hovercraft service from Ramsgate harbour to Calais using the passenger-carrying Saunders-Roe Nautical 4 (SR.N6) craft.

7th   The United Kingdom asks the UN Security Council for authority to use force to stop oil tankers that violate the oil embargo against Rhodesia. Authority is given on the 10th April.

11th   The Marquess of Bath, in conjunction with Jimmy Chipperfield, opens Longleat Safari Park. This becomes the first drive-through park outside Africa.

15th   Time magazine uses the phrase "Swinging London" for the first time.

19th   Ian Brady and Myra Hindley go on trial at Chester Crown Court charged with three Moors Murders.

30th   A regular hovercraft service begins over the English Channel. This was discontinued in 2000 due to competition from the Channel Tunnel. Liverpool win the Football League First Division title for the second time in three seasons.

The opening of Longleat Safari Park

MAY

3rd   Swinging Radio England and Britain Radio start broadcasting on AM from the same ship anchored off the south coast of England but in international waters.

6th   Moors Murderers Ian Brady and Myra Hindley are sentenced to life imprisonment.

12th   African members of the UN Security Council say that the British army should blockade Rhodesia.

14th   Everton defeat Sheffield Wednesday 3-2 in the FA Cup final at Wembley Stadium.

16th   A strike is called by the National Union of Seamen. It eventually ends on the 16th July.

18th   Home Secretary Roy Jenkins announces that the number of police forces in England and Wales will be cut to 68.

26th   Guyana gains independence from the United Kingdom.

JUNE

6th	BBC1 television sitcom Till Death Us Do Part begins its first series.
23rd	The Beatles go to the top of the British singles charts for the 10th time with the song Paperback Writer.
29th	Barclays Bank introduces the first British credit card the Barclaycard.

JULY

3rd   31 arrests made after a protest against the Vietnam War outside the US embassy turns violent.

12th   Zambia threatens to leave the Commonwealth because of British peace overtures to Rhodesia.

14th   Gwynfor Evans becomes the member of Parliament for Carmarthen after his by-election victory. Evans is Plaid Cymru's first MP.

15th   A ban on black workers at Euston railway station is overturned.

16th   Prime Minister Harold Wilson flies to Moscow to try to start peace negotiations over the Vietnam War. The Soviets reject his ideas.

20th   The Government announce the start of 6-month wage and price freeze.

26th   Lord Gardiner issues the Practice Statement in the House of Lords. It states that the House is not bound to follow its own previous precedent.

30th   England beats West Germany 4-2 to win the 1966 World Cup at Wembley. Geoff Hurst scored a hat-trick with the other English goal scored by Martin Peters. The game attracted an all-time record UK television audience of more than 32,000,000.

Captain Bobby Moore is presented with the World Cup Trophy from the Queen

AUGUST

1st	Everton sign Blackpool's World Cup winning midfield player Alan Ball, Jr. for a national record fee of £110,000.
2nd	Spanish government forbids overflights of British military aircraft.
4th	The Kray Twins are questioned in connection with a murder in London.
5th	The Beatles release the album Revolver.
10th	George Brown succeeds Michael Stewart as Foreign Secretary.
12th	Three policemen are shot dead whilst sitting in their patrol car in Braybrook Street, Shepherd's Bush, West London.
18th	The Tay Road Bridge across the Firth of Tay was officially opened by the Queen Mother. At around 2,250m (1.4 miles) it is one of the longest road bridges in Europe and replaced the old Tay ferry.
29th	The Beatles played their very last concert at Candlestick Park in San Francisco, California. The Park's capacity was 42,500 but only 25,000 tickets were sold leaving large sections of unsold seats.

The opening of the Tay Road Bridge

SEPTEMBER

3rd	30 year old footballer John Nicholson, a Doncaster Rovers centre-half who previously played for Port Vale and Liverpool, is killed in a car crash.
5th	Selective Employment Tax is imposed.
15th	Britain's first Polaris submarine HMS Resolution is launched at Barrow-in-Furness.
17th	The Oberon-class submarine HMCS Okanagan is launched at Chatham Dockyard and is the last warship to be built there.
19th	Scotland Yard arrests Ronald "Buster" Edwards who is suspected of being involved in the 1963 Great Train Robbery.
27th	The British Motor Corporation (BMC) makes 7,000 workers redundant.
30th	The Bechuanaland Protectorate in Africa achieves independence from the U.K. as Botswana.

OCTOBER

4th   The British Crown colony Basutoland, which was established in 1884, becomes independent and takes the name Lesotho.

18th   The Ford Cortina MK2 is launched.

20th   437,229 people are reported to be unemployed in Britain which is a rise of some 100,000 on Septembers figures.

21st   144 people (of which 116 were children) are killed by collapsing coal spoil tip in Aberfan, South Wales.

22nd   British spy George Blake escapes from Wormwood Scrubs prison and is next seen in Moscow.

       Spain demands that United Kingdom stop military flights to Gibraltar - Britain says "no" the following day.

25th   Spain closes its Gibraltar border to vehicular traffic.

NOVEMBER

5th   Thirty-eight African states demand that the United Kingdom use force against Rhodesian government.

9th   The Rootes Group launches the Hillman Hunter, a four-door family saloon to compete with the Austin 1800, Ford Cortina and Vauxhall Victor.

16th   The television drama Cathy Come Home is broadcast by the BBC. Viewed by 25% of the British population it is considered influential on public attitudes to homelessness.

24th   Unemployment rises to 531,585.

30th   Barbados achieves independence from the United Kingdom.

DECEMBER

1ˢᵗ	Prime Minister Harold Wilson and Rhodesian Prime minister Ian Smith negotiate onboard HMS Tiger in the Mediterranean.
12ᵗʰ	Harry Roberts, John Duddy and John Whitney are sentenced to life imprisonment (each with a recommended minimum of thirty years) for the murder of three West London policemen in August. Roberts was eventually released in 2014 after spending 48 years in jail, Duddy died in Parkhurst prison in 1981 and Whitney was released in 1991 (and was himself murdered by his flatmate in 1999).
20ᵗʰ	Harold Wilson withdraws all his previous offers to Rhodesian government and announces that he agrees to independence only after the founding of a black majority government.
22ⁿᵈ	Rhodesian Prime minister Ian Smith declares that he considers that Rhodesia is already a republic.
31ˢᵗ	Thieves steal 8 paintings worth millions of pounds from Dulwich Art Gallery in London. They included paintings by Rembrandt, Rubens, Gerrit Dou and Adam Elsheimer.

HMS Tiger hosts talks between the Prime Minister and the Rhodesian Prime Minister

OTHER EVENTS FROM 1966

- Centre Point, a 32-floor office building at St Giles Circus in London is completed. Designed by Richard Seifert for property speculator Harry Hyams it will remain empty for around a decade.
- The London School of Contemporary Dance founded.
- Mathematician Michael Atiyah wins a Fields Medal.
- The motorway network continues to grow as the existing M1, M4 and M6 motorways are expanded. New motorways emerge in the shape of the M32 linking the M4 with Bristol and the M74 near Hamilton in Scotland.
- Japanese manufacturer Nissan begins importing its range of Datsun branded cars to the United Kingdom.

UK Personalities

Born In 1966

Richard Paul "Rick" Astley
6th February 1966

Singer, songwriter, musician and radio personality. He is widely known for his 1987 song "Never Gonna Give You Up" which was a No. 1 hit single in 25 countries. Astley is the only male solo artist to have his first 8 singles reach the Top 10 in the UK. By the time of his retirement in 1993 Astley had sold approximately 40 million records worldwide.

Bennet Evan "Ben" Miller
24th February 1966

Comedian, actor and director. He is best known as one half of comedy double act Armstrong and Miller with Alexander Armstrong. Miller and Armstrong have written and starred in the Channel 4 sketch show Armstrong and Miller as well as the BBC sketch show The Armstrong and Miller Show. Miller was to studying for a PhD at Cambridge in solid state physics when he abandoned completion of his thesis to pursue a career in comedy.

Alan Roger Davies
6th March 1966

Stand-up comedian, writer and actor. Best known for playing the title role in the BBC mystery drama series Jonathan Creek since 1997 and for appearing as the permanent panellist on QI since 2003.

Gregory Leonard George Barker
8th March 1966

A Conservative Party politician. Barker became the MP for Bexhill and Battle in 2001 after the retirement of the sitting Conservative MP Charles Wardle. In May 2010 he was appointed Minister of State for Energy and Climate Change.

Alastair Preston Reynolds
13th March 1966

Reynolds is a science fiction author who specialises in dark hard science fiction and space opera. He earned his PhD from the university of St Andrews, Fife and in 1991 went to work for the European Space Research and Technology Centre (part of the European Space Agency). In 2004 he left this to pursue writing full-time.

Andrew Richard Rosindell
17th March 1966

Conservative politician and MP for the Romford constituency in Greater London. Rosindell is also the international director of leading Eurosceptic think tank the European Foundation and chairman of the All Party Parliamentary Flags & Heraldry Committee.

Nigel Howard Clough
19th March 1966

Former football player and manager. Clough made his most notable contribution as a player at Nottingham Forest where he appeared in over 400 matches. During this time he scored 131 goals making him the second highest scorer in the club's history. In the 1990's Clough was also capped by England 14 times.

Mark Fraser Williams
24th March 1966

Welsh Liberal Democrat politician and former deputy headteacher. Williams is the Member of Parliament for the Ceredigion constituency which he gained from Plaid Cymru in 2005. He sits on the Welsh Affairs Select Committee and in 2006 he became a Shadow Minister for Wales under Sir Walter Menzies Campbell.

Roger Anthony Black, MBE
31st March 1966

Retired athlete who during his career won individual silver medals in the 400 metres sprint at both the Olympic Games and World Championships, two individual gold medals at the European Championships and 4x400 metres relay gold medals at both the World and European Championships. Since retiring from athletics he has worked as a television presenter and motivational speaker.

Christopher James "Chris" Evans
1st April 1966

Presenter, businessman and producer for radio and television. His break came with the Channel 4 television show The Big Breakfast which made him a star. With slots on the Radio 1 Breakfast Show and TFI Friday by 2000 he was the UK's highest paid entertainer according to the Sunday Times Rich List. In 2005 he moved to BBC Radio 2 and he also now presents The One Show on a Friday.

Sharon Hodgson
1st April 1966

Labour Party politician who has been the Member of Parliament for Washington and Sunderland West since 2010. She was previously the MP for Gateshead East and Washington West.

Edward Paul "Teddy" Sheringham, MBE
2nd April 1966

Football manager and former player who is currently the manager of Stevenage. Sheringham played as a forward during a 24-year professional career for teams such as Millwall, Nottingham Forest, Tottenham Hotspur, Manchester United and West Ham United. In 2001 he was named both the PFA Players' Player of the Year and FWA Footballer of the Year.

Lisa Stansfield
11th April 1966

Singer, songwriter and actress. Her career began in 1980 when she won the singing competition Search for a Star. Stansfield has won numerous awards including Brit Awards, Ivor Novello Awards, Billboard Music Award, World Music Award, ASCAP Award, Women's World Award, Silver Clef Awards and DMC Awards. She has sold over twenty million albums worldwide.

Samantha Karen "Sam" Fox
15th April 1966

Singer, songwriter, actress and former glamour model. Her career began in 1983 at the age 16 when she began appearing on Page 3 of The Sun. During this time she became the most popular pin-up girl of her era. In 1986 she launched her pop-music career with her debut single "Touch Me (I Want Your Body)" which went to Number 1 in 17 countries.

Philip Clive Roderick "Phil" Tufnell
29th April 1966

Former cricketer turned television personality. A slow left-arm orthodox spin bowler he played 42 Tests (taking 121 Test wickets) and 20 One Day International matches for England. He also played for Middlesex from 1986 retiring in 2002. Tufnell has built on his popularity with several television appearances including They Think It's All Over, A Question of Sport, Strictly Come Dancing and winning I'm a Celebrity... Get Me Out of Here!

Jonathan David Edwards, CBE
10th May 1966

Former triple jump Olympic, World, Commonwealth and European champion. He has held the world record in the event since 1995. Following his retirement as an athlete Edwards has worked as a sports commentator and presenter for the BBC. Formerly a devout Christian he renounced his faith in 2007. In 2011 he was elected President of Wenlock Olympian Society and was also a member of the London Organising Committee for the 2012 Olympic and Paralympic Games.

Helena Bonham Carter, CBE
26th May 1966

Actress who made her name in a television adaptation of K. M. Peyton's A Pattern of Roses before her film debut as the titular character in Lady Jane. She is also known for her roles in films such as A Room with a View, Fight Club, The King's Speech and for playing Bellatrix Lestrange in the Harry Potter series. She has frequently collaborated with director Tim Burton and is two-time Academy Award nominee.

William David Wiggin
4th June 1966

Conservative Party politician, MP and a former Shadow Minister for Agriculture & Fisheries. He held the seat of Leominster from the 2001 election until 2010 when the seat was abolished. Wiggin now holds the seat of North Herefordshire having been elected in 2010. Wiggin has strong roots in the constituency and is a passionate campaigner for local issues such as agriculture, rural broadband and better rail links.

Tamsin Margaret M. Greig
12th July 1966

Actress who played Fran Katzenjammer in Black Books and Dr. Caroline Todd in Green Wing. Other roles include Alice Chenery in BBC One's comedy drama Love Soup, Debbie Aldridge in BBC Radio 4's soap opera The Archers, Miss Bates in the 2009 BBC version of Jane Austen's Emma and Beth Hardiment in the 2010 film version of Tamara Drewe. Greig is also an acclaimed stage actress and she won a Laurence Olivier Award for Best Actress in 2007 for Much Ado About Nothing.

Diana Ruth Johnson
25th July 1966

Labour Party politician who has been the MP for Hull North since 2005. Johnson was the Parliamentary Under Secretary of State with responsibility for Schools in the Department for Children, Schools and Families from 2009 until 2010 as well as being an Assistant Whip for the Government.

Shirley Ann Manson
26th August 1966

Singer, songwriter, musician and actress. She is best known internationally as the lead singer of the alternative rock band Garbage. For much of her international career Manson commuted between her home city of Edinburgh and the United States to record with Garbage. Manson gained media attention for her forthright style, rebellious attitude and distinctive voice.

David William Donald Cameron
9th October 1966

Politician who was first elected to Parliament in the 2001 general election for the Oxfordshire constituency of Witney. He was promoted to the Opposition front bench two years later and rose rapidly to become head of policy co-ordination during the 2005 general election campaign. He won the Conservative leadership election in 2005 and has served as the Prime Minister of the United Kingdom since 2010.

Tony Alexander Adams, MBE
10th October 1966

Manager and former football player. Adams spent his entire 22 year playing career as a defender at Arsenal. He is considered one of the greatest Arsenal players of all time by the club's own fans and was included in the Football League 100 Legends. With Arsenal he won four top flight division titles uniquely captaining a title-winning team in three different decades.

Steve Valentine
26th October 1966

Actor, musician and magician who has performed on stage and screen. He is best known for his role as the eccentric Nigel Townsend on NBC's crime drama Crossing Jordan and as Harry Flynn in the critically acclaimed PlayStation 3 game Uncharted 2: Among Thieves. Additionally he was the voice of Alistair in Bioware's Dragon Age franchise and he starred in the Disney XD sitcom I'm in the Band as Derek Jupiter.

Jeremy Richard Streynsham Hunt
1st November 1966

A Conservative Party politician Hunt was elected at the 2005 general election to represent the constituency of South West Surrey. When the Conservatives and Liberal Democrats formed a coalition following the 2010 general election Hunt was appointed Secretary of State for Culture, Olympics, Media and Sport.

Gordon James Ramsay, Jr., OBE
8th November 1966

Chef and restaurateur whose restaurants have been awarded a total of 16 Michelin Stars. His signature restaurant, Restaurant Gordon Ramsay in Chelsea, London, has held 3 Michelin stars since 2001 (Ramsay was the first Scottish chef ever to have won three Michelin stars). Ramsay is known for presenting TV shows such as the series Hell's Kitchen, The F Word and Ramsay's Kitchen Nightmares.

Ian Richard Kyle Paisley, Jr.
12th December 1966

Paisley is the Member of Parliament for North Antrim and has been in office since 2010. Previously he was a member of the Northern Ireland Assembly for North Antrim from 1998 to 2010. Paisley is a member of the Democratic Unionist Party (DUP) and the son of the DUP's founder Revd Dr. Ian Paisley.

Dennis Frank Wise
16th December 1966

Former football player, manager and Executive Director of Football at Newcastle United. Wise played as a central midfielder and was noted for his aggressive and highly competitive style of play. In a career spanning over 20 years he played for Wimbledon, Leicester City, Millwall, Southampton, Coventry City and most notably as the captain of Chelsea.

Martin Offiah, MBE
29th December 1966

Former professional rugby league footballer who played throughout the 1980s, 1990s and 2000s. As a winger he played for Great Britain and England and because of his running speed is nicknamed "Chariots" Offiah after the film Chariots of Fire. Offiah scored 501 tries during his rugby league career making him the third-highest try scorer of all time. Since retiring he has provided commentary for Sky Sports and worked as a player agent.

Sporting Winners

BBC Sports Personality
Bobby Moore - Football

Moore and Eusebio with their awards

In 1966 Bobby Moore captained England to a famous World Cup win at Wembley against Germany and capped the year off by being named BBC Sports Personality of the Year. In keeping with the recognition of World Cup achievement the England team were also named Team of the Year and Portugal striker Eusebio, the tounaments top scorer with 9 goals, claimed the Overseas Personality award.

Moore captained West Ham United for more than ten years as well as being the captain of the England World Cup winning team. He is widely regarded as one of the greatest defenders of all time and was cited by Pelé as the greatest defender that he had ever played against. He won a total of 108 England caps during his career which was a national record for outfield player. This record wasn't beaten until the 28th March 2009 when David Beckham gained his 109th cap.

FIVE NATIONS RUGBY
WALES

Position	Nation	Played	Won	Draw	Lost	For	Against	Points
1	Wales	4	3	0	1	34	26	6
2	France	4	2	1	1	35	18	5
3	Scotland	4	2	1	1	23	17	5
4	Ireland	4	1	1	2	24	34	3
5	England	4	0	1	3	15	36	1

The 1966 Five Nations Championship was the thirty-seventh series of the rugby union Five Nations Championship. Including the previous incarnations as the Home Nations and Five Nations, this was the seventy-second series of the northern hemisphere rugby union championship. Ten matches were played between the 15th January and 26th March.

Results:

15/01/1966	Scotland		3-3		France	Edinburgh
15/01/1966	England		6-11		Wales	London
29/01/1966	France		11-6		Ireland	Paris
05/02/1966	Wales		8-3		Scotland	Cardiff
12/02/1966	England		6-6		Ireland	London
26/02/1966	France		13-0		England	Paris
26/02/1966	Ireland		3-11		Scotland	Dublin
12/03/1966	Ireland		9-6		Wales	Dublin
19/03/1966	Scotland		6-3		England	Edinburgh
26/03/1966	Wales		9-8		France	Cardiff

CALCUTTA CUP WINNERS

SCOTLAND

The Calcutta Cup was first awarded in 1879 and is the rugby union trophy awarded to the winner of the match (currently played as part of the Six Nations Championship) between England and Scotland.

FORMULA 1 - BRITISH GRAND PRIX
JACK BRABHAM

Jack Brabham wins the British Grand Prix driving a Brabham BT19

The 1966 British Grand Prix was held at Brands Hatch on the 16th July. It was the fourth round of the 1966 World Championship and the 21st British Grand Prix (the second to be held at Brands Hatch). It was held over 80 laps of the 2.65 mile circuit giving a total race distance of 212 miles. The race was won for the third time by Australian driver Jack Brabham in his Brabham BT19. New Zealander Denny Hulme finished second in his Brabham BT20 which was a first 1–2 win for the Brabham team. The pair finished a lap ahead of third placed British driver Graham Hill in his BRM P261 and ended a streak of 4 consecutive wins by Jim Clark at the British Grand Prix.

1966 FORMULA 1 SEASON REVIEW

Drivers Champion – Jack Brabham
International Cup (Manufacturers) - Brabham-Repco

	Race	Circuit	Date	Winning Driver
1	Monaco Grand Prix	Monaco	22/05/1966	Jackie Stewart
2	Belgium Grand Prix	Spa-Francorchamps	12/06/1966	John Surtees
3	French Grand Prix	Reims	03/07/1966	Jack Brabham
4	British Grand Prix	Brands Hatch	16/07/1966	Jack Brabham
5	Dutch Grand Prix	Zandvoort	24/07/1966	Jack Brabham
6	German Grand Prix	Nürburgring	07/08/1966	Jack Brabham
7	Italian Grand Prix	Monza	04/09/1966	Ludovico Scarfiotti
8	U.S. Grand Prix	Watkins Glen	02/10/1966	Jim Clark
9	Mexican Grand Prix	Magdalena Mixhuca	23/10/1966	John Surtees

The 1966 Formula One season, which was the 17th season of FIA Formula One racing, featured the World Championship of Drivers and the International Cup for F1 Manufacturers. The two titles were contested concurrently over a nine race series which commenced on the 22nd May and ended on the 23rd October. The season also included a number of non championship races for Formula One cars.

Grand National
Anglo

The 1966 Grand National was the 120th running of this world famous horse race. It took place at Aintree Racecourse near Liverpool on the 26th March 1966. 50/1 winner Anglo won by 20 lengths and was trained by Fred Winter and ridden by Tim Norman (who had been injured in a car accident just two days earlier). Of the 47 horses who took part only 12 actually completed the race.

	Name	Jockey	Age	Weight	Odds
1st	Anglo	Tim Norman	8	10st 0lbs	50/1
2nd	Freddie	Pat McCarron	9	11st 7lbs	11/4
3rd	Forest Prince	Gerry Scott	8	10st 8lbs	100/7

12 Finished
14 Fell / 2 Unseated / 2 Brought Down / 2 Baulked / 11 Pulled Up / 4 Refused

Epsom Derby
Charlottown

Charlottown, an English thoroughbred racehorse and sire, was ridden to victory by Australian jockey Scobie Breasley. In a career which lasted from 1965 until 1967 he ran ten times and won seven races. The Derby Stakes is Britain's richest horse race and the most prestigious of the country's five Classics. First run in 1780 this Group 1 flat horse race is open to three year old thoroughbred colts and fillies. It is run at Epsom Downs in Surrey over a distance of one mile, four furlongs and 10 yards (2,423 metres) and is scheduled for early June each year.

1966 WORLD CUP - ENGLAND

The 1966 FIFA World Cup was the eighth staging of the World Cup and was held in England from 11th to the 30th July. England beat West Germany 4–2 in the final to win their first World Cup and become the third World Cup host to win the tournament after Uruguay in 1930 and Italy in 1934. The 1966 Final which was held at Wembley Stadium was the last to be broadcast in black and white. The tournament held a 28-year FIFA record for the largest average attendance until it was surpassed by the United States in 1994.

THE FINAL

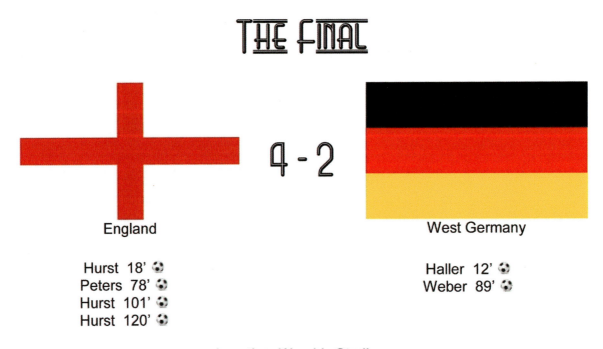

4 - 2

England   West Germany

England	West Germany
Hurst 18' ⚽	Haller 12' ⚽
Peters 78' ⚽	Weber 89' ⚽
Hurst 101' ⚽	
Hurst 120' ⚽	

Location: Wembly Stadium
Attendance 96,024
Referee: Gottfried Dienst (Switzerland)

FA CUP WINNERS
EVERTON

Everton	3-2	Sheffield Wednesday
Trebilcock 59' ⚽		McCalliog 4' ⚽
Trebilcock 64' ⚽		Ford 57' ⚽
Temple 74' ⚽		

Referee: Jack Taylor

The 1966 FA Cup Final took place on the 14th May 1966 at Wembley Stadium. It was the 94th year, 85th final (due to World Wars) and the 38th to be played at Wembley. It was contested between Everton, who were the first team since Bury FC in 1903 to reach an FA Cup Final without conceding a goal in the preceding rounds, and Sheffield Wednesday. The Beatles John Lennon and Paul McCartney were just two of the 100,000 spectators who attended the match.

SNOOKER
JOHN PULMAN

With the agreement of the Billiards Association and Control Council the World Snooker Championship was revived by Rex Williams on a challenge basis after a six-year absence in 1964. The 1957 World Champion John Pulman played two challenge matches in 1966 winning both. The tournament reverted to a knock-out tournament in 1969.

John Pulman	39-12	Fred van Rensburg
John Pulman	5-2	Fred Davis

The British Open – Golf

Jack Nicklaus

Jack Nicklaus of the United States won the British Open at Muirfield, which was played between the 6th and 9th July, by 1 stroke to take the Claret Jug and prize money of £2100. By winning Nicklaus became only the fourth player to win all four major professional championships.

The Open Championship, or simply The Open (often referred to as the British Open), is the oldest of the four major championships in professional golf and was established in 1860 at Prestwick Golf Club in Scotland. Held in the United Kingdom it is administered by The R&A and is the only major outside the United States. The Open is currently the third major of the calendar year following The Masters and the U.S. Open and preceding the PGA Championship. The winner is presented with The Golf Champion Trophy better known by its popular name of the Claret Jug.

Heavyweight Boxing Ali vs Cooper

Henry Cooper fought against Muhammad Ali for The Ring and WBC World Heavyweight titles on the 21st May at Arsenal Stadium, Highbury, London. Cooper knocked Ali down in the 4th round but controversially Ali's trainer Angelo Dundee illegally held smelling salts under Ali's nose in an effort to revive his man. Cooper started the 5th round aggressively attempting to make good his advantage but a recovered Ali effectively countered. Cooper was hit high on the face with a hard right which opened a severe cut under his eye and referee Tommy Little was forced to stop the fight and Ali won by TKO.

Henry Cooper was the first (and is today one of just three people) to twice win the public vote for the BBC Sports Personality of the Year Award and is thus far the only boxer ever to be awarded a knighthood.

WIMBLEDON

Mens Singles Champion - Manolo Santana - Spain
Ladies Singles Champion - Billie Jean King - U.S.

The 1966 Wimbledon Championships took place on the outdoor grass courts at the All England Lawn Tennis and Croquet Club in Wimbledon, London. The tournament ran from the 20th June until the 1st July. It was the 80th staging of the Wimbledon Championships and the third Grand Slam tennis event of 1966.

BRITISH EMPIRE & COMMONWEALTH GAMES

The 8th British Empire and Commonwealth Games were held in Kingston, Jamaica from 4th to 13th August 1966 covering 110 events in 10 sports. 34 Nations participated with a total of 1,316 althletes and officials.

Medals table - Top 7 countries;

Rank	Nation	Gold	Silver	Bronze	Total
1	England	33	24	23	80
2	Australia	23	28	22	73
3	Canada	14	20	23	57
4	New Zealand	8	5	13	26
5	Ghana	5	2	2	9
6	Trinidad & Tobago	5	2	2	9
7	Pakistan	4	1	4	9

TOP 10
SINGLES 1966

No.1   Jim Reeves   Distant Drums
No.2   Frank Sinatra   Strangers In The Night
No.3   The Beatles   Yellow Submarine / Eleanor Rigby
No.4   The Four Tops   Reach Out I'll Be There
No.5   Nancy Sinatra   These Boots Are Made For Walkin'
No.6   The Walker Brothers The Sun Ain't Gonna Shine Anymore
No.7   Tom Jones   Green Green Grass Of Home
No.8   The Kinks   Sunny Afternoon
No.9   The Troggs   With A Girl Like You
No.10 Manfred Mann   Pretty Flamingo

Jim Reeves
Distant Drums

Label:	Written by:	Length:
RCA Victor	Cindy Walker	2 mins 46 secs

James Travis "Jim" Reeves (20th August 1923 - 31st July 1964) was an American country and popular music singer-songwriter. Known as "Gentleman Jim" his songs continued to chart for many years after his death. He is a member of both the Country Music and Texas Country Music Halls of Fame.

Frank Sinatra
Strangers In The Night

Label:	Written by:	Length:
Reprise Records	Kaempfert / Singleton / Snyder	2 mins 35 secs

Francis Albert "Frank" Sinatra (12th December 1915 - 14th May 1998) was an American singer, actor, director and producer. Sinatra is one of the best-selling music artists of all time having sold more than 150 million records worldwide. He was honored at the Kennedy Center Honors in 1983, was awarded the Presidential Medal of Freedom by Ronald Reagan in 1985 and the Congressional Gold Medal in 1997. Sinatra was also the recipient of eleven Grammy Awards including the Grammy Trustees Award, Grammy Legend Award and the Grammy Lifetime Achievement Award.

③ The Beatles
Yellow Submarine / Eleanor Rigby

Label:	Written by:	Length:
Parlophone	Lennon / McCartney	2m 40s / 2m 11s

The Beatles were an English rock band that formed in Liverpool in 1960. With members John Lennon, Paul McCartney, George Harrison and Ringo Starr they became widely regarded as the greatest and most influential act of the rock era. They have had more number-one albums on the British charts and sold more singles in the UK than any other act. They have received ten Grammy Awards, an Academy Award for Best Original Song Score and fifteen Ivor Novello Awards. Collectively included in Time magazine's compilation of the twentieth century's 100 most influential people they are the best-selling band in history with estimated sales of over 600 million records worldwide. The group was inducted into the Rock and Roll Hall of Fame in 1988 with all four being inducted individually as well from 1994 to 2015.

④ The Four Tops
Reach Out I'll Be There

Label:	Written by:	Length:
Tamla Motown	Holland / Dozier / Holland	2 mins 58 secs

The Four Tops are an American vocal quartet from Detroit, Michigan who helped to define the city's Motown sound of the 1960s. The group's repertoire has included soul music, R&B, disco, adult contemporary, doo-wop, jazz and show tunes.

⑤ Nancy Sinatra
These Boots Are Made For Walkin'

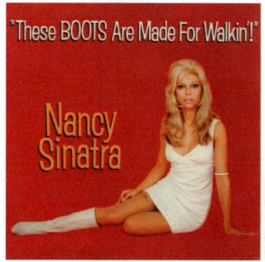
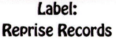

Label:	Written by:	Length:
Reprise Records	Lee Hazelwood	2 mins 42 secs

Nancy Sandra Sinatra (born on the 8th June 1940) is an American singer and actress. She is the daughter of the late singer and actor Frank Sinatra and is widely known for this 1966 transatlantic number 1 hit. Sinatra also had a brief acting career in the mid-60s including a co-starring role with Elvis Presley in the movie Speedway and with Peter Fonda in The Wild Angels. In the comedy film Marriage on the Rocks, Frank and Nancy Sinatra played a fictional father and daughter.

⑥ The Walker Brothers
The Sun Ain't Gonna Shine Anymore

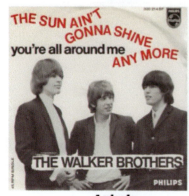

Label:	Written by:	Length:
Philips Records	Bob Crewe / Bob Gaudio	3 mins 02 secs

The Walker Brothers were an American pop group of the 1960s and 1970s that included Scott Engel, John Maus and Gary Leeds. After moving to Britain in 1965 they provided a unique counterpoint to the British Invasion by achieving much more success in the United Kingdom than in their home country.

Tom Jones
Green, Green Grass Of Home

Label:	Written by:	Length:
Decca	Claude Putman	3 mins 02 secs

Sir Thomas Jones Woodward, OBE (born 7th June 1940) is a Welsh singer known by his stage name **Tom Jones**. He became one of the most popular vocalists to emerge from the mid-1960s. Since then he has sung nearly every form of popular music including pop, rock, R&B, show tunes, country, dance, soul and gospel. Jones has sold over 100 million records and had thirty-six Top 40 hits in the United Kingdom and nineteen in the United States.

The Kinks
Sunny Afternoon

Label:	Written by:	Length:
Pye Records	Ray Davies	3 mins 30 secs

The Kinks were an English rock band formed in Muswell Hill, North London by brothers Dave Davies and Ray Davies in 1963 with Pete Quaife. The band were part of the British Invasion of the US and are recognised as one of the most important and influential rock groups of the era. In the UK the group had seventeen Top 20 singles and five Top 10 albums. In 1990 the original four members of The Kinks were inducted into the Rock & Roll Hall of Fame (as well as the UK Music Hall of Fame) in November 2005.

9 The Troggs
With A Girl Like You

Label:	Written by:	Length:
Fontana Records	Reg Presley	2 mins 05 secs

The Troggs (originally called The Troglodytes) are an English rock band formed in Andover, Hampshire in 1964. They have had a number of hits in the United Kingdom and the United States with their most famous singles being the U.S. chart-topper "Wild Thing", "With a Girl Like You" and "Love Is All Around" (they each sold over 1 million copies).

10 Manfred Mann
Pretty Flamingo

Label:	Written by:	Length:
His Master's Voice	Mark Barkan	2 mins 31 secs

Manfred Mann were an English beat, rhythm and blues and pop band (with a strong jazz foundation). They were named after their keyboardist and were chart regulars in the 1960s. Manfred Mann were also the first south-of-England-based group to top the US Billboard Hot 100 during the British invasion. Three of the band's most successful singles, "Do Wah Diddy Diddy", "Pretty Flamingo" and "Mighty Quinn" all made it to number 1 in the British Singles Chart.

TOP 5
FILMS 1966

1. The Bible: In The Beginning...
2. Hawaii
3. Who's Afraid Of Virginia Woolf?
4. The Sand Pebbles
5. A Man For All Seasons

OSCARS

Best Picture: A Man For All Seasons

Best Actor: Paul Scofield
(A Man For All Seasons)
Best Actress: Elizabeth Taylor
(Who's Afraid Of Virginia Woolf?)

THE BIBLE: IN THE BEGINNING...

Directed by: John Huston

Runtime: 174 minutes

Extravagant production of the first 22 chapters of the book of Genesis covering Adam and Eve, Noah and the Flood, the story of Nimrod King of Babel and Abraham and Isaac. This elaborate Hollywood retelling of the Bible stories is narrated by the film's director John Huston.

Gross $34,900,023

STARRING

Michael Parks
Born: 4th April 1940

Character:
Adam

American actor and singer who was born Harry Samuel Parks. He has appeared in over 50 films and has made frequent television appearances but is still probably best known for his work in recent years with filmmakers such as Quentin Tarantino, Robert Rodriguez and Kevin Smith.

Ulla Bergryd
Born: 25th July 1942

Character:
Eve

Swedish born Bergryd was picked from obscurity for the role in this film. She has had one or two other bit parts in other films but never had any further success as an actress. She went on to become a senior lecturer at the Institute of Sociology at the University of Stockholm in Sweden.

Richard Harris
Born: 1st October 1930
Died: 25th October 2002

Character:
Cain

Irish actor, singer, theatrical producer, film director and writer. He appeared on stage and in films such as This Sporting Life, Camelot, Unforgiven, Gladiator and the first two Harry Potter films. Harris won a Golden Globe for Best Actor in Camelot (1968) and a Grammy in Jonathan Livingston Seagull (1973). He was twice nominated for an Academy Award for Best Actor.

TRIVIA

Goofs

Before they get into the Ark one of Noah's daughters-in-law is seen to be wearing a modern day bra under her tunic.

At the end of an early dialog between Sarah and her handmaid we see that the back of her dress is held together with a modern day zip.

Interesting Facts

This was one of the first mainstream American films to feature male and female nudity (albeit artfully filmed in a light and shadow style) in the Garden of Eden sequences. Reportedly neither Michael Parks nor Ulla Bergryd used body doubles for these scenes.

When God talks to Noah (played by director John Huston) it is actually the voice of John Huston speaking to himself.

CONTINUED

Interesting Facts Filming of The Tower of Babel sequence was disrupted when Egyptian extras staged a rock-throwing riot.

Strangely director John Huston was a self-professed atheist.

Unusually there are no opening credits except for the title of the film. While this may be standard practice for blockbusters today it was very rarely that way in the 1960s.

John Huston's original idea was to have Charlie Chaplin play Noah. However Chaplin didn't much like the idea of appearing in a picture directed by someone else and Huston wound up playing the role himself.

It took John Huston five years to complete the film.

Ava Gardner (who played Sarah) and George C. Scott (Abraham) had a brief but stormy affair during the making of this film. At one point he was said to have kicked down the door of her hotel suite in a drunken rage.

Hawaii

Directed by: George Roy Hill
Runtime: 189 minutes

James Michener's novel reaches the screen.

THE MIRISCH CORPORATION PRESENTS

JULIE ANDREWS
MAX VON SYDOW
RICHARD HARRIS
in THE GEORGE ROY HILL-WALTER MIRISCH PRODUCTION of
"HAWAII"

Abner Hale, a rigid and humorless New England missionary, marries the beautiful Jerusha Bromley and takes her to the exotic island kingdom of Hawaii intent on converting the natives. But the clash between the two cultures is too great and instead of understanding there comes tragedy.

Gross $34,562,222

STARRING

Julie Andrews
Born: 1st October 1935

Character:
Jerusha Bromley

Dame Julia Elizabeth Andrews is an English film and stage actress, singer, author, theatre director and dancer. Andrews, a former child actress and singer, appeared on the West End in 1948 and made her Broadway debut in 1954. Her film debut was in Mary Poppins (1964) for which she won the Academy Award for Best Actress. A year later in The Sound of Music (1965) she won the Golden Globe Award for Best Actress in a Musical.

Max von Sydow
Born: 10th July 1929

Character:
Rev. Abner Hale

A Swedish-French actor. He has starred in many films and had supporting roles in dozens more in many languages including Swedish, Norwegian, English, Italian, German, Danish, French and Spanish. Von Sydow received the Royal Foundation of Sweden's Cultural Award in 1954, was made a Commandeur des Arts et des Lettres in 2005 and was named a Chevalier de la Légion d'honneur in 2012.

Richard Harris
Born: 1st October 1930
Died: 25th October 2002

Character:
Capt. Rafer Hoxworth

Irish actor, singer, theatrical producer, film director and writer. He appeared on stage and in films such as This Sporting Life, Camelot, Unforgiven, Gladiator and the first two Harry Potter films. Harris won a Golden Globe for Best Actor in Camelot (1968) and a Grammy in Jonathan Livingston Seagull (1973). He was twice nominated for an Academy Award for Best Actor.

TRIVIA

Goofs

In the opening scene, which is set in 1818, Jerusha is said to be 22 but a later shot of her gravestone has her born in 1799.

During the initial journey from New England to Hawaii there is a heavy rainstorm but the skies are bright blue with no rain clouds.

Interesting Facts

This film was responsible for launching the career of Bette Midler. She can be seen in the crowd as an extra playing a seasick passenger aboard a ship listening to the preacher played by Max von Sydow. Midler was also hired for a small speaking role and went to Los Angeles to film these scenes in the studio. Her scenes were cut from the final film however Midler used the money she earned to move to New York and her career took off.

Rock Hudson was the first actor suggested for the role of Captain Rafer Hoxworth which was eventually played by Richard Harris.

CONTINUED

Interesting Facts
Jocelyne LaGarde who played Malama Kanakoa in the film is the only performer in Academy Award history to be nominated for the only performance ever given. LaGarde had never acted before and never acted again in her entire life.

The real life sons of actor Max von Sydow, Henrik and Clas, both played his son Micah at different ages during the film. Henrik played a 7-year-old Micah and Clas played a 12-year-old Micah.

The fictional character of Malama in James A. Michener's book and subsequently in this movie was based on Queen Ka'ahumanu the actual ruler of Maui at the time of the missionaries' arrival to the islands.

Quotes
[Reading from a proclamation to her subjects]
Queen Malama: Next law: Everyone will love Jesus.

[Later]
Queen Malama: Too much law make people mad.

WHO'S AFRAID OF VIRGINIA WOOLF?

Directed by: Mike Nichols - Runtime: 131 minutes

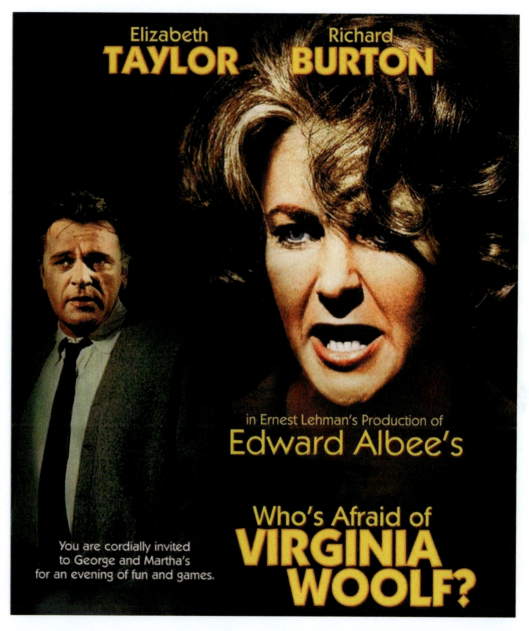

George and Martha are a middle aged married couple whose charged relationship is defined by vitriolic verbal battles which underlies what seems like an emotional dependence upon each other. This verbal abuse is fueled by an excessive consumption of alcohol. Martha invites Nick and Honey over for a nightcap and they get caught up in George and Martha's games of needing to hurt each other and everyone around them.

Gross $28,000,000

STARRING

Elizabeth Taylor
Born: 27ᵗʰ February 1932
Died: 23ʳᵈ March 2011

Character:
Martha

Dame Elizabeth Taylor was a British-American actress who from her early years as a child star with MGM became one of the greatest screen actresses of Hollywood's Golden Age. She won her first Oscar for Best Actress for BUtterfield 8 in 1960. Later, after playing the title role in Cleopatra (1963), she married her co-star Richard Burton. They appeared together in 11 films including Who's Afraid of Virginia Woolf? for which Taylor won a second Academy Award.

Richard Burton, CBE
Born: 10ᵗʰ November 1925
Died: 5ᵗʰ August 1984

Character:
George

Welsh stage and cinema actor noted for his mellifluous baritone voice and his great acting talent. Burton was nominated seven times for an Academy Award without ever winning. He was though a recipient of BAFTA, Golden Globe and Tony Awards for Best Actor. In the mid-1960s Burton ascended into the ranks of the top box office stars and by the late 1960s was one of the highest paid actors in the world.

Gerorge Segal
Born: 13ᵗʰ February 1934

Character:
Nick

American actor and musician. Segal became popular in the 1960s and 1970s for playing both dramatic and comedic roles. He was nominated for the Academy Award for Best Supporting Actor for his performance in Who's Afraid of Virginia Woolf? and won two Golden Globe Awards for his performance in A Touch of Class. Some of his other acclaimed roles were in Where's Poppa? (1970), Blume in Love (1973) and California Split (1974).

TRIVIA

Goofs

The first scene of George and Martha entering the living room shows a 3 light floor lamp in the corner of the room. The next scene of the area shows a single globe lamp hanging from the wall. The single globe lamp remains through out the rest of the film.

When revealing the secret of his wife's money near the rope swing George refills Nick's drink nearly full and it instantly becomes almost empty as Nick takes the glass back.

Interesting Facts

Who's Afraid of Virginia Woolf? became the first motion picture in cinema history to be nominated in every Academy Award category for which it was eligible.

Interesting Facts

Every credited member of the cast received an Academy Award nomination and this is the only film in which a two pairs of married characters have competed for Oscars.

Elizabeth Taylor gained nearly 30 pounds to play the role of the middle-aged Martha in this film.

Richard Burton celebrated his 40th birthday on the set of the film where spouse Elizabeth Taylor presented him with a white 1966 Oldsmobile Toronado.

This is the first film in which the British Board of Film Classification (BBFC) allowed use of the word "bugger" in its dialogue.

On the 18th July 1966 police seized this film and arrested the manager of a cinema in Nashville for contravening a municipal order that banned films of an obscene nature.

Costing $7.5 million this was the most expensive black & white movie ever made in the United States. Elizabeth Taylor, Richard Burton and writer Edward Albee's combined salaries / fees were $2,350,000 not including percentages ($1,100,000 for Taylor, $750,000 for Burton and $500,000 for Albee).

THE SAND PEBBLES

Directed by: Robert Wise
Runtime: 182 minutes

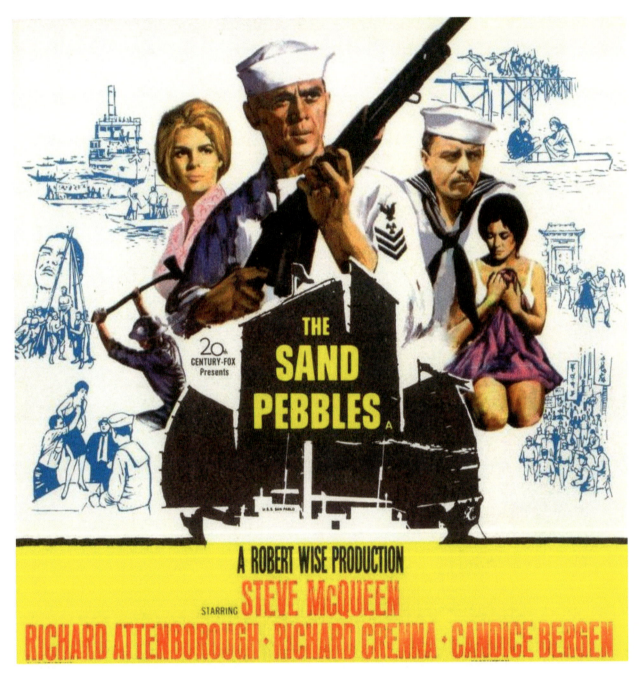

Engineer Jake Holman arrives aboard the gunboat U.S.S. San Pablo (nicknamed the Sand Pebble) assigned to patrol a tributary of the Yangtze in the middle of exploited and revolution-torn 1926 China. On board the Sand Pebble Holman must deal with a captain whose wants often do not match what Holman can carry out. Hostility towards the gunboat's presence reaches a climax when the boat must crash through a river-boom and rescue missionaries upriver at China Light Mission.

Gross $30,017,647

STARRING

Steve McQueen
Born: 24th March 1930
Died: 7th November 1980

Character:
Jake Holman

American actor often referred to as "The King of Cool". McQueen received an Academy Award nomination for his role in The Sand Pebbles. His most popular films include The Blob, The Thomas Crown Affair, Bullitt, The Getaway and Papillon. Other all-star films he appeared in include The Magnificent Seven, The Great Escape and Towering Inferno. By 1974 he had become the highest-paid movie star in the world.

Richard Attenborough
Born: 29th August 1923
Died: 24th August 2014

Character:
Frenchy Burgoyne

English actor, film director, producer, entrepreneur and politician. As a film director and producer Attenborough won two Academy Awards for Gandhi in 1983. During his career he also won a total of four BAFTA Awards and four Golden Globe Awards. As an actor he is perhaps best known for his roles in Brighton Rock, The Great Escape, 10 Rillington Place, Miracle on 34th Street and Jurassic Park.

Candice Bergen
Born: 9th May 1946

Character:
Shirley Eckert

American actress and former fashion model. She made her big screen debut in 1966 and was nominated for the Golden Globe Award for New Star of the Year for her role in this film. Her biggest success was for her part as the title character on the CBS sitcom Murphy Brown for which she has won five Emmy Awards and two Golden Globe Awards as Best Actress in a TV Comedy.

TRIVIA

Goofs

When the San Pablo first gets underway Holman is wearing a clean set of dungarees. In the next shot when he is noticing an engine problem he has on some old worn and dirty dungarees with no undershirt.

Upon seeing the boom in the river the Captain leans forward grabbing the forward handrail. In the next scene he is again seen leaning forward grabbing the forward handrail.

At the fight at the boom the cannon on the USS Sand Pebble has a recoil cylinder on top of the barrel but when fired the barrel doesn't recoil.

Interesting Facts

Steve McQueen got his only nomination for an Academy Award (Best Actor) for his role in this film.

Interesting Facts

This Twentieth Century Fox release marked their switch from their own Cinemascope process to Panavision.

Director Robert Wise was so proud of this film that he held yearly parties with surviving cast members to celebrate it.

There is a credit for 'Diversions by Irving Schwartz' in tribute to a mysterious unknown correspondent whose letters proved a morale booster to cast and crew during trying location work in Hong Kong and Taiwan.

The San Pablo was purpose built for the film in Hong Kong. She was actually powered by diesel engines and the black smoke from the stack came from old tyres and other rubbish fired in a special compartment on the boat.

Pat Boone badly wanted the lead role. He says he believes he didn't get it because director Robert Wise wanted a "real actor" instead of a singer-turned-actor.

Quotes:

Captain Collins: Holman, I'll have you shot as a mutineer!
Jake Holman: Well shoot something!

A MAN FOR ALL SEASONS

Directed by: Fred Zinnermann

Runtime: 120 minutes

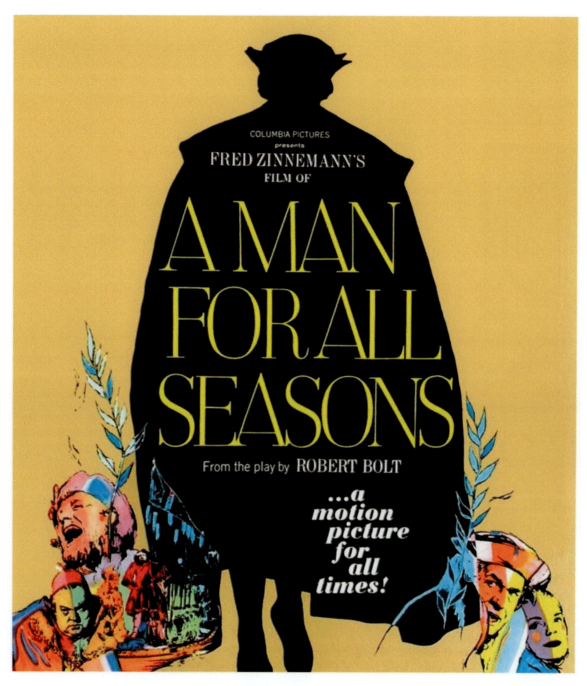

When King Henry VIII seeks a divorce he looks for the support of Sir Thomas More who is a devout Catholic. While More does not agree with the King's desire to divorce he is completely silent in his opposition. His principles are tested however when he also remains silent after the King is named the head of the Church of England and subsequently when Parliament requires all to take an oath of allegiance. More's silence is not sufficient for the King and he is eventually brought to trial.

Gross $28,350,000

STARRING

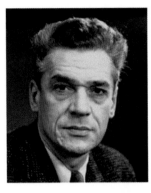

Paul Scofield
Born: 21st January 1922
Died: 19th March 2008

Character:
Thomas More

David Paul Scofield CH CBE was an English actor of stage and screen who was known for his striking presence, distinctive voice and for the clarity and effortless intensity of his delivery. He is regarded as one of the greatest Shakespearean actors of all time. Scofield preferred the stage over film nevertheless he won a BAFTA and the Academy Award for Best Actor for his role in this film.

Wendy Hiller
Born: 15th August 1912
Died: 14th May 2003

Character:
Alice

Dame Wendy Margaret Hiller was an English film and stage actress who enjoyed a varied acting career that spanned nearly sixty years. She was nominated for Academy Award for Best Supporting Actress for her role in this film. Despite many other notable film performances including winning an Oscar for Best Supporting Actress in the film Separate Tables (1958) she chose to remain primarily a stage actress.

Robert Shaw
Born: 1st October 1930
Died: 25th October 2002

Character:
Cromwell

English actor, novelist and playwright. With his menacing mutter and intimidating demeanor he was often cast as a villain. He is best remembered for his performances in From Russia with Love (1963), A Man for All Seasons (1966) for which he was nominated for Best Supporting Actor, The Sting (1973), The Taking of Pelham One Two Three (1974), Jaws (1975) and Force 10 from Navarone (1978).

TRIVIA

Goofs

When Sir Thomas More enters the room to first answer charges before Secretary Cromwell a chandelier with electric lights is visible in the background.

Wolsey says it is known that Catherine of Aragon was barren. In fact by this point she had already given birth several times but only one child had survived, Mary, who went on to become Mary I, Queen of England and Ireland.

When King Henry visits Thomas More's house and steps off the boat he steps into mud and makes light of it. When his retinue follow their feet and leggings are already muddy from a previous take.

Interesting Facts

Truckloads of styrofoam were ordered to simulate a snowy landscape but when it was actually delivered it started to snow.

Charlton Heston lobbied heavily for the role of Thomas More but was never seriously considered by the producers. Heston would go on to play More in several stage productions of the play and ultimately film a television production of it in 1988.

According to Orson Welles (who played Cardinal Wolsey) he had director Fred Zinnemann removed from the set and directed his scenes himself.

Richard Burton turned down the role of Sir Thomas More.

Paul Scofield won the 1962 Tony Award (New York City) for Actor in a Drama for "A Man for All Seasons" and recreated his role in this filmed production.

Vanessa Redgrave was originally lined up to play Margaret (eventually played by Susannah York) but she had theater commitments. Instead she agreed to do an unpaid cameo as Anne Boleyn on the condition that it remain unbilled.

The film won six Academy Awards including Best Film, Actor, Director, Cinematography, Screenplay and Costume Design.

Quotes

The Duke of Norfolk: Your life lies in your own hands, Thomas, as it always has.
Sir Thomas More: Is that so, My Lord? Then I'll keep a good grip on it.

THE COST OF LIVING

COMPARISON CHART

	1966 Price	Equivalent Amount Today (taking into account inflation)	2015 Price
3 Bedroom House	£4,800	£82,996	£209,428
Weekly Income	£10 13s 4d	£184.44	£498
Pint Of Beer	1s 2d	£1.01	£3.31
Cheese (lb)	3s 11d	£3.39	£3.10
Bacon (lb)	5s	£4.32	£4.17
The Beano	3d	22p	£2.20

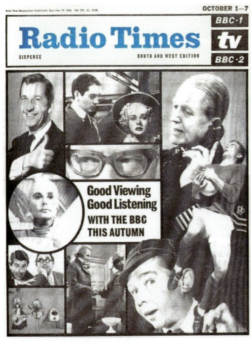

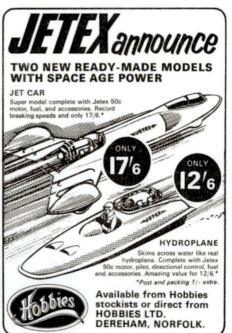

GROCERIES

Freece Toothpaste	1s 10½d
Anadin (100)	7s 3d
Fine Fair Pure Dairy Butter (lb)	2s 10d
Stork Margarine (per ½lb)	9½d
Robertsons Mince Meat	1s 5d
Fray Bentos Corned Beef (tin)	3s
Heinz Tomato Ketchup (12oz)	1s 6d
Branston Pickle	1s 7d
Findus Steakburgers (large packet)	2s 9d
Eskimo Fish Fingers (large)	2s
Canned Tomatoes	11½d
Heinz Baked Beans (8oz)	7d
Surprise Peas (serves 3)	1s 1½d
Ambrosia Creamed Rice Pudding (tin)	10½d
Quaker Sugar Puffs	1s 11½d
Robertsons Strawberry Jam	1s 9½d
Pepsi Cola (per can)	9½d
Lyons Premium Tea (4oz)	1s 5½d
Maxwell House Instant Coffee (2oz)	2s 3d
Ginger Nut Biscuits	10d
Mintoes Mint Sweets (large pack)	1s 6d
Sunsilk Shampoo	2s
Close-Up Deodorant	4s 11d
Glen Toilet Rolls (twin pack)	1s 4d
Pears Bath Soap	1s 4d
Daz Washing Powder (giant size)	2s 9d
3 Hands Washing Up Liquid	10d

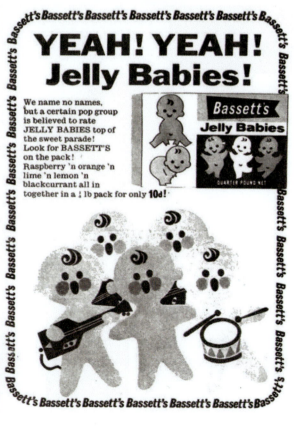

CLOTHES

Women's Clothing

Swears & Wells Mink Fur Coat	79gns
Womens Casual Jacket	59s 8d
Dorothy Perkins Summer Dresses	29s 11d
Hipster Skirt	19s 11d
Criss-Cross Corset	19s 11d
Marks & Spencers Stockings	3s 11d

Men's Clothing

Burtons Mens Suit	£9 19s 6d
Nylon Shirt	39s 6d
Ties	6s 11d
Socks	7s 11d
Pyjamas	29s 11d

Everybody's wild about 'Crimplene'

The gentlest-mannered jersey with the highest spirits in the world is made of 'Crimplene'. Soft, smooth, or crisp, or chunky, 'Crimplene' makes lovely sense of dresses, always keeps its shape.

Stay happy all summer in this zippy little, hippy little, two-piece-looking dress. It's not only the style, it's not only the wash-and-look-new 'Crimplene' talent, it's the sheer *comfort* of this supple, feather-light jersey . . . By Lapidus of Sweden in (you've guessed it) 'Crimplene' jersey. Style 8959. About 13½ gns.

'Crimplene' is the jersey that always keeps its shape. (It's pure 'Terylene'—that's why!)

'Crimplene' TERYLENE

Raleigh RSW 14 Childs Bicycle	£19 3s 3d
Luxury Dolls Pram	76s 6d
17in Pretty Doll	27s 6d
Batman Batcopter	19s 11d
Top Of The Pops Drum Set	57s 6d
Train Set	19s 9d

ELECTRICAL ITEMS

Philips Popmaster Portable Radio	£7 19s 6d
Tricity Luxury Cooker	66gns
Frigidaire 4.6 cu.ft Refridgerator	42½gns
Hoovermatic De-Luxe Washing Machine	65gns
Morphy Richards Steam Iron (Super)	£5 14s 3d
Ricoh Auto Zoom Cine Camera	15gns
Polaroid Swinger Instant Camera (b&w)	£9 19s 6d
Philishave Cordless Shaver	£5 5s 0d

OTHER PRICES

Hillman Hunter 90mph Family Car	£837
Gallon Of Petrol	5s 5d
Costa Blanca – Skytours Holiday In Benidorm	from 32gns
Seagers Cream Sherry	12s 6d
Benson & Hedges Sterling Cigarettes (20)	4s 7d
Golden Virginia Tobacco (½oz)	3s 0½d
TV Times	6d

If you're thinking of ferrying yourself abroad this year, travel in a car that's made to measure distances. The Austin A110.

Long trips, either at home or abroad, can present their problems: planning an unfamiliar route, booking hotels, where to board out the dog.

When you own an Austin A110, your car, at least, is not one of them.

Everything about the A110, is designed for distances. The six-cylinder, three-litre engine is the kind of power unit that actually thrives on activity. So head for the nearest motorway and settle back. The more miles you cover, the more effortlessly your A110 responds. (Try this long-distance runner in a *sprint*. Some sportscars don't have this kind of go!)

The A110, you will soon discover, is a restful car to travel in. Much of the credit goes to the suspension (anti-sway telescopic shock absorbers are the latest development). The seats are the kind that let you sink in: the Super de Luxe version has the fully reclining type. And you travel in *silence*, thoroughly insulated from the engine and the road.

There are three different models: Mark II Saloon, Saloon de Luxe and Super de Luxe—with Borg Warner automatic transmission available as an optional extra on all three. The most expensive of them offers walnut and leather finishes and twin picnic tables in the back.

So if time is of the essence you can enjoy lunch in your A110—and feel completely at home with the cuisine!

AUSTIN

By Appointment to
Her Majesty The Queen
Motor Car Manufacturers
The Austin Motor
Company Limited

BMC

THE **BRITISH** MOTOR
CORPORATION LTD.

A110 Mark II Saloon
(including £173.8.9 P.T.)—£998.8.9
Saloon de Luxe
(including £186.19.7 P.T.)—£1,076.19.7
Super de Luxe
(including £193.4.7 P.T.)—£1,113.4.7

BACKED BY BMC SERVICE-EXPRESS. EXPERT. EVERYWHERE
THE AUSTIN MOTOR CO. LTD. LONGBRIDGE, BIRMINGHAM   BMC EXPORT SALES LTD. BIRMINGHAM AND 41-46 PICCADILLY, LONDON W.1

THE MONEY

Money Conversion Table

Old Money		Equivalent Today
Farthing	¼d	0.1p
Half Penny	½d	0.21p
Penny	1d	0.42p
Threepence	3d	1.25p
Sixpence	6d	2.5p
Shilling	1s	5p
Florin	2s	10p
Half Crown	2s 6d	12.5p
Crown	5s	25p
Ten Shillings	10s	50p
Pound	20s	£1
Guinea	21s	£1.05

Printed in Great Britain
by Amazon